# Maine Agriculture Collection

## Apples

## Farming: Then and Now

## The Maine Potato

## Harvest the Sea

## Pancakes: Blueberries and Maple Syrup

**Homeschoolers of Maine**
P.O. Box 159, Camden, ME 04843
Telephone: 207.763.2880  Email: homeschl@midcoast.com
www.homeschoolersofmaine.org

# Table of Contents

Each unit study contains its own individual table of contents.  There you will find specifics for that individual study.

# INTRODUCTION

Homeschoolers of Maine (HOME) is a statewide 501(c)3 non-profit, ministry-based organization, and was founded on the belief that all families have a God-given and constitutional right and responsibility to direct the education of their children, regardless of their educational philosophy or religious affiliation.

Our mission is to:
**Preserve** parent-led home education
**Protect** homeschool freedoms, and
**Promote** safe and healthy learning environments.

Thank you for supporting Homeschoolers of Maine by choosing one of our carefully constructed unit study bundles for your student.

In each bundle, HOME strives to provide at least one question or activity within each of the required subject areas: Math, Language Arts, Social Studies, Science, Health, Physical Education, Maine Studies, Computer, Library Skills, and Fine Arts. Bible is also included, and occasionally Foreign Language, for those who would like to cover those additional areas. This helps to illustrate how a study on a single subject can cover multiple required areas.

These studies are not a conclusive study of the subject but is intended to spark the student's interest by asking them questions and providing them with basic direction in which to begin pursuing their study of the subject. In most cases, it does not contain answers to the questions asked. This is intentional. Our unit studies are designed to help students explore, discover and develop their own perspective on various subjects that are of interest to them.

Students should in no way be confined to the questions and activities contained here. If their level of interest widens or veers off in another direction, encourage them to follow their passion.

# OVERVIEW

## Apples

As you enter the fall season, be sure to check out this unit study. Are you planning your own field trip to a local apple orchard in your area? This study is a great way to cover the topic of apples across the curriculum. You'll even take a brief look at mission work.

## Farming: Then and Now

In this study, students will explore farming, past and present. The study will look at various things related to farming in general, while encouraging a visit to your local farm, farmer's market or farm stand. It is an opportunity to move beyond online games like Minecraft into the realm of real life farming.

## The Maine Potato

In this study, the student will explore the potato, a staple Maine crop. It's a chance to see it as more than a part of our dinner menu. See what your children know before you begin, and be amazed by what they learn through the exploration and discovery process of this study.

## Harvest the Sea

In this study, students will explore the subject of lobsters and seaweed as agricultural resources in Maine.

## Pancakes: Blueberries and Maple Syrup

This study allows students to explore Maine's maple sap and blueberry harvests, combining them into the fun theme of pancakes.

# Apples

**Revised 2020**

# Table of Contents

## Before You Begin

Sometimes it can be challenging to figure out how to show progress when a student is working on a unit study. Before you begin this study, ask the student to give you a brief narrative of what they already know about the subject of this HOME unit study. Write this out for younger students. Have older students write it out for themselves, here. When you finish the study, there is a page at the end entitled, *What I Learned,* for students to write down new things that they learned during the study. The comparison of these two pages can be used for portfolio reviews to document that progress in learning was made by the student.

_____
_____
_____
_____
_____
_____
_____
_____
_____
_____
_____
_____
_____
_____
_____
_____
_____
_____
_____
_____
_____
_____
_____
_____
_____

Date Begun: _____

# 12 Apple Fun Facts

**Did you know that…**

… the crabapple is the only apple native to North America?

…the science of apples is called pomology?

…apples are a member of the rose family?

…it takes the energy of 50 leaves to produce one apple?

…apples have 5 seed pockets called carpels, which contain seeds?

…different apples have different numbers of seeds?

…apples ripen six to ten times faster at room temperature than if they are refrigerated?

….a bushel of apples weighs 42 pounds and will yield 20 – 24 quarts of applesauce?

…..it takes about 36 apples to make a gallon of cider?

… Americans eat about 21 pounds of fresh apples per person each year?

…apple trees need bees to pollinate the flowers to form fruit, they are not self-pollinating?

…25% of an apple's volume is air, which is why they can float?

…the first apple trees were planted by Pilgrims in Massachusetts Bay Colony?

# BIBLE

Deuteronomy 32:10, Proverbs 7:2 and Psalm 27:8 each include a phrase using the word apple.

Copy the phrase below.

_____

_____


What do you think the phrase means?

_____

_____

_____


Copy Psalm 17:8 below and memorize it.

_____

_____

_____


Read Genesis 3:1-6 The fruit of the tree of the knowledge of good and evil is often depicted as being an apple. Write out your argument supporting whether you believe it was an apple or not. Younger students can narrate, with parents writing for them.

_____

_____

_____

_____

_____

_____

_____

www.homeschoolersofmaine.org

# MATH

If it takes 36 apples to make a gallon of cider, and your family drank one gallon of cider per week, then how many apples would you need to make enough cider for your family for one month? _____

One year? _____

Every apple core has five carpels (seed pockets). Each carpel contains a different number of seeds. Estimate how many seeds you think an apple will have, and then cut the apple open and count them. Do this with several apples. Chart your findings.

|  | My estimate | Actual number of seeds |
|---|---|---|
| Apple 1 |  |  |
| Apple 2 |  |  |
| Apple 3 |  |  |
| Apple 4 |  |  |

Measure and weigh several apples of several different varieties. Chart your findings.

|  | Type of Apple | Weight |
|---|---|---|
| Apple 1 |  |  |
| Apple 2 |  |  |
| Apple 3 |  |  |
| Apple 4 |  |  |

# LANGUAGE ARTS

## Apples Word Search

Find the words from the list below in the puzzle. If you don't know the meaning of a word, look it up in the dictionary or online.

```
E D W B T O E E N N C L G U G
M C U X U J M I C T F A V O B
F L Q O T P V J P T L Z T M Y
P M D R I S R R B D X Q R I Q
T Q E R P N I E F D D F E I V
Q Q E T A N I L L O P Y B N E
X Q S T S H S E L F Z G R V I
P M Z K L A C P J K E J T R Z
K R I A I L M R L R H W O E M
P Y V Q E N J A O H C K Y T N
F R K E L N U C R F M A Q P F
P S B Q C G U W L L U L H L K
V P J E A Q P U Q Z K G Y Z Q
Q M N C R Q P M U R U I J X K
O I D J T W M V J L B N H A M
```

| carpel | core | empire | flesh | orchard |
|--------|------|--------|-------|---------|
| pollinate | seed | skin | stem | |

Explore poetry styles at www.kathimitchell.com/poemtypes.html.  Then write a poem about an apple, apple tree, or orchard.

_____
_____
_____
_____
_____
_____
_____
_____
_____

Illustrate your poem in the box below.

**NOTES:**

Read a book about apples and write a book report. You will find a list of books in the Additional Resources section at the end of this study.

# BOOK REPORT FORM

**Date Read:** _____

**Book Title:** _____

**Author:** _____

**Number of Pages:** _____

**Fiction or non-fiction?** _____

**Briefly describe what the book was about?**

_____

_____

_____

_____

_____

**Where does the story take place?**

_____

_____

_____

**What did you like best/least about this book?**

_____

_____

_____

_____

**Draw a picture from the story here.**

## SOCIAL STUDIES

Research missionary John Chapman. His birthday was September 26, 1774. What was he noted for in relationship to apples?

_____

_____

_____

_____

_____

_____

Map the travels of missionary John Chapman.

# SCIENCE

Bob for apples.  Why do apples float?

_____

_____

_____

_____

_____

Draw and label the parts of an apple.

Next time you have an apple to eat, save the seeds.  Sprout and plant the seeds and grow an apple tree.
Keep a journal tracking how long it takes the seeds to sprout and to grow.

# COMPUTER/LIBRARY SKILLS

You will use the internet and/or your local library for a great deal of the research for this unit study.

List the various resources you used during the course of your study.


Source Title                                                                 Type of Media

_____

_____

_____

_____

_____

_____

_____

_____

_____

_____

_____

_____

_____

_____

_____

_____

_____

_____

_____

_____

_____

_____

_____

_____

_____

_____

_____

_____

## HEALTH/PHYSICAL EDUCATION

Make pink applesauce, naturally.  You will find the recipe at http://www.familyfeedbag.com/2011/08/canning-pink-applesauce.html

"An apple a day keeps the doctor away" is something your great grandmother may have said.

Research the health benefits of apples and explain why this saying may or may not be true.

_____

_____

_____

_____

_____

_____

_____

_____

Find a healthy snack recipe that includes apples. Make it for your family.

What did you make?

_____

_____

_____

_____

_____

Learn how to dehydrate apples. Make apple rings, and dehydrate them in your oven or in a food dehydrator.

**FINE ARTS**

Look up classic paintings that have apples in them. *Plate of Apples* by Cezanne; *Still Life with Apples* by Van Gogh; *Still Life with Apples and Grapes* by Monet are all possibilities. Create your own drawing or painting with apples.

Using two apples, cut each apple in half in opposite directions. Using red, green and yellow tempera paint, make apple print cards to send to a relative or friend, telling them about your trip to the apple orchard.

# MAINE STUDIES

How many varieties of apples are grown in Maine? _____

Which one is your favorite? _____

Approximately how many bushels of apples are harvested each year in Maine? _____

When does apple picking season typically begin? _____

What is the only type of apple tree that is native to Maine? _____

Plan ahead to attend one of Maine's Annual Apple Festivals in September.

What two Apple Festivals take place in Maine?

1. _____

2. _____

Which Maine town has the word "apple" in its name? _____

What county is it in? _____

When was the town established? _____

How did the town get its name? _____

Are there any apple orchards in this town? _____

**FIELD TRIP**

Visit a local orchard and pick apples.  You can find a list of orchards in Maine at

www.maineapples.org.

# Field Trip Form

**Date:** _____

**Destination:** _____

**Purpose:** _____

**List the types of apples you picked:**

_____

_____

_____

**Which type do you like best?** _____

**Did you learn anything new?** _____

_____

_____

_____

**Draw a picture showing something you did or learned.**

## What I Learned

In this section, ask the student to narrate what they learned that they didn't know when they began this study. What new discovery did they make during the study? What did they enjoy most? What do they know now that they didn't know before? These are all good questions to ask, if the student needs prompting.

_____
_____
_____
_____
_____
_____
_____
_____
_____
_____
_____
_____
_____
_____
_____
_____
_____
_____
_____
_____
_____
_____
_____
_____
_____
_____

Date Completed: _____

# Additional Resources:

**Books**

*True Tale of Johnny Appleseed* by Margaret Hodges

*Johnny Appleseed* by Reeve Lindbergh

*Snow White* (Grimms fairy tale)

*How do Apples Grow* by Guilio Maestro

*Apples* by Gail Gibbons

The Apple Star: Story and Activities on Teachers Pay Teachers

INTERNET RESOURCES:

enchantedlearning.com/school/usa/people/appleseedindex.shtml

# Farming: Then and Now

# Table of Contents

# Before You Begin

Sometimes it can be challenging to figure out how to show progress when a student is working on a unit study. Before you begin this study, ask the student to give you a brief narrative of what they already know about the subject of this HOME unit study. Write this out for younger students. Have older students write it out for themselves, here. When you finish the study, there is a page at the end entitled, *What I Learned,* for students to write down new things that they learned during the study. The comparison of these two pages can be used for portfolio reviews to document that progress in learning was made by the student.

_____
_____
_____
_____
_____
_____
_____
_____
_____
_____
_____
_____
_____
_____
_____
_____
_____
_____
_____
_____
_____
_____
_____
_____
_____

Date Begun: _____

# BIBLE

Take a moment to consider, before Walmart and Hannaford or Shaw's, where did people get the food they ate?

_____

_____

_____

_____

_____

In the Creation Story in the book of Genesis, find the verse where it tells about God creating the plants to be food. Write it out.

_____

_____

_____

_____

Read Genesis 2:15, and Genesis 3:17—19. What do these verses have to do with farming?

_____

_____

_____

_____

_____

_____

Read Exodus 23:10-11 What was God's command to the people concerning sowing the land? Is this practice still used today? _____

_____

_____

_____

_____

What lessons about farming can we learn from the following verses?

Ecclesiastes 11:4 _____

_____

_____

Proverbs 27:34-35 _____

_____

_____

Proverbs 20:4 _____

_____

_____

Proverbs 21:5 _____

_____

_____

1 Corinthians 3:8 _____

_____

_____

Deuteronomy 8:10 _____

_____

_____

Leviticus 23:22 _____

_____

_____

In the book of Jeremiah, the author instructs people to build houses and plant gardens. What is the lesson in this that God has for us?

_____

_____

_____

_____

_____

www.homeschoolersofmaine.org

# MATH

How many square feet are in an acre? _____

Would an acre of land be enough for a garden to feed your family for a year? _____

Open a green bean and count the seeds.  Estimate how many beans one plant produces.  Multiply that by the number of the seeds in the bean.  Approximately how many seeds for future plants would one bean plant produce?

_____

_____

Is math important for farmers and farming?  Consider all the ways that a farmer uses math concepts and skills in his or her daily farming operation, and list them here.

_____

_____

_____

_____

How many eggs does it take to feed your family one breakfast? _____

If you were to raise chickens, and each chicken laid one egg per day, how many chickens would you need in order to feed your family for a month? _____

How much milk does a dairy cow produce in a day? _____

How many ounces is that? _____

Calculate that by the number of days in a month.  How much milk would you have? _____

If each member of your family drank 2 glasses of milk each day (16 oz), how much milk would they drink in a month? _____

If you had one dairy cow, would it produce enough milk for your family? _____

Using what you have learned about farmers and farming, create a math story problem and give it to a sibling or friend to solve.

_____

_____

_____

_____

Read *Henry's Map* by David Eliot. Where is your favorite farm-stand or farmer's market located? How many miles is it from your home? How do you get there, and what do you see along the way? Create a directional picture map from your house to the farm-stand or market. ("Maps" will vary depending on age. Encourage children to think about roads, signs, buildings, trees, etc.)

_____

_____

_____

_____

_____

**LANGUAGE ARTS**

Consider reading one or more of the following books during the course of this study.  They can be read independently by the student or as a family read-aloud. Complete the  book report form below.

\_\_\_\_\_ *Charlotte's Web* by E.B.White

\_\_\_\_\_ *Ox Cart Man* by Donald Hall

\_\_\_\_\_ *A Year at Maple Hill Farm* by Alice Provensen

\_\_\_\_\_ *James Herriot's Treasury for Children* by James Herriot

---

# BOOK REPORT FORM

**Date Read:** _____

**Book Title:** _____

**Author:** _____

**Number of Pages:** _____

**Who are the main characters in the story?**

_____

_____

_____

**What is a story setting?  Think carefully about the setting of one of the books or stories that you chose to read, and create it using art materials, clay, small toys and blocks, etc.**

**What did you like best/least about this book?**

_____

_____

_____

_____

**Draw or post a picture of the story setting you created.**

Define the farming related terms below, then arrange them in alphabetical order.

Irrigation _____

_____

Till _____

_____

Harvest _____

_____

Combine _____

_____

Agriculture _____

_____

Produce _____

_____

Cultivator _____

_____

Organic _____

_____

Fallow _____

_____

1. _____

2. _____

3. _____

4. _____

5. _____

6. _____

7. _____

8. _____

9. _____

# SOCIAL STUDIES

Consider visiting the following websites as sources of information on farming in Maine.

_____ Get Real Get Maine – www.getrealmaine.com
_____ Maine Farmland Trust – www.mainefarmlandtrust.org
_____ Forever Farms – www.foreverfarms.org
_____ Maine State Grange – www.mainestategrange.org
_____ Maine Association of Agricultural Fairs – www.mainefairs.org
_____ Maine's Cooperative Extension 4-H Program – http://extension.umaine.edu/4h/

Choose one of these organizations to investigate and learn more about their important role in the farming community in Maine. Record what you learned.

_____
_____
_____
_____
_____
_____
_____
_____
_____
_____
_____
_____
_____
_____
_____
_____

What plants and animals are common to farms that we think of as being native, but were actually brought by settlers to this country.

_____
_____
_____
_____
_____
_____
_____
_____
_____

Create a Farming Timeline. Research and compare how farming was done when our country was founded, and how inventions and technology have changed it over time. What is farming like today? How is it similar to and different from what farming was then?

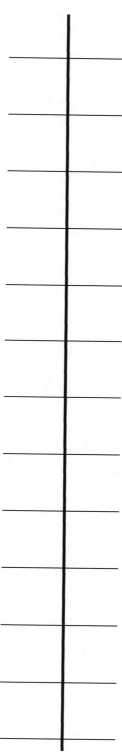

**NOTES:**

Read a biography of Thomas Jefferson.  What were his contributions to agriculture?  What is the difference between a farm and a plantation?

_____
_____
_____
_____
_____
_____
_____
_____

How many of the US Presidents have farmed?  Was it before, during or after the time that they were in office?  What are some of the things they grew?

_____
_____
_____
_____
_____
_____
_____
_____
_____
_____
_____
_____
_____
_____
_____
_____
_____
_____

# SCIENCE

Create a written timeline that reflects the history of milk collection, from an old fashioned pail and milk can, through the delivery of milk to the door in glass jars, to today's modern milk collection and distribution. Study how milk collection and preservation has changed through history.

_____
_____
_____
_____
_____
_____
_____
_____
_____
_____
_____

While animals may be raised for food, oftentimes they are also used to help the farmer with his crops. Explore what types of animal manure is used to fertilize crops and whether or not it must "age" before it can be used.

_____
_____
_____
_____
_____

Use a copy of *Roots, Shoots, Buckets and Boots* by Sharon Lovejoy, to learn about creating specialty gardens, like a pizza garden where you can grow most of the ingredients necessary top a pizza.

_____
_____
_____
_____
_____

What does GMO stand for? What is the relevance to GMO's in farming today? Do you think it is wise for scientists and farmers to alter food from the way God created it? Why or why not?

_____
_____
_____
_____
_____

Learn about soil.

Maine has 70 soil types! What is the name of the Maine state soil?  What does the name mean and why do you think it was chosen to be the state soil?

_____
_____
_____
_____
_____

What type of soil is best for farming?  What can you do if the soil around your home isn't good for growing food in?

_____
_____
_____
_____
_____

Learn about composting.  Build a compost box and compost food scraps from your kitchen to create your own fertilizer for gardening.

_____
_____
_____
_____
_____

How does compost help your garden grow?  _____
_____
_____
_____

Besides food scraps, what other things can be composted for use in gardens?

_____
_____
_____
_____

## HEALTH/PHYSICAL EDUCATION

Does tetanus/lockjaw really come from rusty nails or from horses.  Read the article at the link below.  Share whether you agree or disagree with the article and why.

https://steemit.com/vaccines/@canadian-coconut/truth-about-tetanus-infection-and-the-vaccine

_____

_____

_____

_____

_____

_____

What is pasteurization?  When did it first become a widespread practice?  Do you think it is beneficial or not?

_____

_____

_____

_____

_____

_____

What is the difference between organic and non-organic food?  Why is this important when purchasing food?

_____

_____

_____

_____

_____

_____

_____

Be sure to keep track of any time you spend gardening and add it to your physical educational log for your portfolio.  You may also be interested in HOME's unit study "*HOME Grown Gardens*" for further study.

# COMPUTER/LIBRARY SKILLS

You will use the internet and/or your local library for a great deal of the research for this unit study. List the various resources you used during the course of your study.

Source Title                                                                    Type of Media

_____

_____

_____

_____

_____

_____

_____

_____

_____

_____

_____

_____

_____

_____

_____

_____

_____

_____

_____

_____

_____

_____

_____

_____

_____

_____

_____

_____

## FINE ARTS

The fiber from some farm animals and plants are used in creating art or art mediums. Maine's Fiber Frolic is the first weekend in June in Windsor. Plan on attending and learning more about different fibers and the source they come from.

Learn about artist Dahlov Ipcar, who lived on a dairy farm in Georgetown, Maine. Plan a trip to the Farnsworth Museum in Rockland, Maine to see her work. Discuss how farm life may have influenced the subject matter of many of her paintings. Read *One Horse Farm*, written and illustrated by Ipcar.

Watch the YouTube video at the link below and choose one of the animals to draw in the box below.
https://www.youtube.com/watch?v=LNdt-6h7WTM

# MAINE STUDIES/FIELD TRIP

What are the main crops grown in Maine? _____

Approximately how much of Maine is farmland? _____

Do some research on Oakhurst, a Maine company that provides milk to local grocery stores. When was it founded and by whom? Where is it located? What is the company's slogan? What other facts did you learn?

_____

_____

_____

_____

_____

_____

_____

_____

_____

What is the path milk takes to get from the farm to your table?

_____

_____

_____

_____

_____

_____

_____

_____

www.homeschoolersofmaine.org

**FIELD TRIP**

Using the Get Real, Get Maine website (www.getrealmaine.org) locate a farm near you and contact them to see if they are open to visitors.  If they are, plan a trip to visit and learn how the farm runs.

Open farm day is the 4th Sunday of July. Check out the website here for farms that will be open to visitors. https://www.maine.gov/dacf/ard/market_promotion/open_farm_day.shtml#:~:text=Open%20Farm%20Day%20is%20the,throughout%20the%20State%20of%20Maine!

## Field Trip Form

**Date:** _____

**Destination:** _____

**Purpose:** _____

**List the farms you visited:**

_____

_____

_____

**Was it a farm that raised animals, or vegetables or both?**

_____

**Did you learn anything new from your visit?** _____

_____

_____

_____

_____

**Draw a picture showing something you did or learned.**

# What I Learned

In this section, ask the student to narrate what they learned that they didn't know when they began this study. What new discovery did they make during the study? What did they enjoy most? What do they know now that they didn't know before? These are all good questions to ask, if the student needs prompting.

_____

_____

_____

_____

_____

_____

_____

_____

_____

_____

_____

_____

_____

_____

_____

_____

_____

_____

_____

_____

_____

_____

_____

_____

_____

_____

Date Completed: _____

# The Maine Potato

# Table of Contents

## Before You Begin

Sometimes it can be challenging to figure out how to show progress when a student is working on a unit study. Before you begin this study, ask the student to give you a brief narrative of what they already know about the subject of this HOME unit study. Write this out for younger students. Have older students write it out for themselves, here. When you finish the study, there is a page at the end entitled, *What I Learned,* for students to write down new things that they learned during the study. The comparison of these two pages can be used for portfolio reviews to document that progress in learning was made by the student.

_____
_____
_____
_____
_____
_____
_____
_____
_____
_____
_____
_____
_____
_____
_____
_____
_____
_____
_____
_____
_____
_____
_____
_____

Date Begun: _____

www.homeschoolersofmaine.org

# BIBLE

Depending on the age and maturity of the student, consider having them watch, individually, or as a family, the movie Faith Like Potatoes. Discuss how faith is like growing potatoes. You can use the discussion questions from the Faith Like Potatoes study guide here: https://www.affirmfilms.com/files/FaithLikePotatoes_Guide.pdf

_____

_____

_____

_____

_____

Mr. Potato Head – Use Mr. Potato Head to teach the lesson from 1 Corinthians 12:12 – 27. A lesson plan for this is available at http://freebiblelessons.net/object-lessons/many-parts-one-potato

_____

_____

_____

_____

_____

# MATH

Estimate how many potatoes one potato can produce. Plant a sprouted potato. At the harvest count the number of potatoes it has produced.

_____

_____

_____

_____

_____

In one meal, how many potatoes does your family eat? _____ Using this number, estimate how many potatoes you would need to feed your family for a week_____, a year _____.

What is the favorite way for your family and friends to eat potatoes? Ask at least 10 friends or family which of the four ways they like most. Chart their answers below. Color in the boxes to create a graph.

| Type/#of likes | French Fries | Mashed Potato | Potato Salad | Baked Potato |
|---|---|---|---|---|
| 9 | | | | |
| 8 | | | | |
| 7 | | | | |
| 6 | | | | |
| 5 | | | | |
| 4 | | | | |
| 3 | | | | |
| 2 | | | | |
| 1 | | | | |

Which potato recipe got the most likes? _____ The least? _____

Consider using the book Math *Potatoes: Mind Stretching Brain Food* by Greg Tang for more potato related math activities.

## LANGUAGE ARTS

Have the student compose a journal entry as if they were a potato. What is it like growing under the ground? Being harvested? Do potatoes talk to each other? What happens when they encounter a worm? A grub? What are their thoughts on what happens when they are taken from the ground?

_____

_____

_____

_____

_____

_____

_____

**Have the student write a poem/prose describing a potato.**

_____

_____

_____

_____

_____

**What is your favorite way to eat potatoes? Have your student write directions on how to make their favorite potato recipe. Be sure to include digging up the potato, washing it, peeling it if necessary, etc.**

_____

_____

_____

_____

_____

_____

_____

_____

_____

_____

_____

_____

_____

_____

Read *Spuds* by Karen Hesse and write a book report on it.

# BOOK REPORT FORM

**Date Read:** _____

**Book Title:** _____

**Author:** _____

**Number of Pages:** _____

**Who are the main characters in the story?**

_____

_____

_____

**Where does the story take place?** _____

_____

**What is the main idea of the story?** _____

_____

_____

_____

_____

**Draw or post a picture of the story setting you created.**

## SOCIAL STUDIES

For a little bit of the history of how the potato became popular, consider the brief write up on this website.  https://bible.org/illustration/potato

The story *A Penny for a Hundred* tells of German prisoners of war working in the potato fields in Maine during World War II.  Read the story and share your thoughts.

_____

_____

_____

_____

Where are most of the potatoes in Maine grown? _____

Which state in the United States produces the largest crop of potatoes? _____

Locate the top ten potato producing states on the map below and color them in.

To learn more about the history of potato growing in Maine, when it started, when it peaked, and where it is today, visit the following websites:

http://pinelandpotatoes.com/maine-potato-history/
http://www.newenglandhistoricalsociety.com/flashback-photos-1940-maine-potato-harvest/
https://visitaroostook.com/story/the-maine-potato/vtm233988BCEA57578A7
http://www.mainepotatoes.com/

Write your own brief history of Maine's potato industry.

_____
_____
_____
_____
_____
_____
_____
_____
_____
_____
_____
_____
_____
_____
_____
_____

# SCIENCE

Define the following:

Tuber _____

Potato blight _____

Carbohydrate _____


Fill a five gallon pail with potting soil and fertilizer and plant one or two sprouted potatoes. Research how to grow potatoes. How much water do they need? What is the ideal temperature they need to grow? How long do they grow before they can be harvested? Grow potatoes in a bucket!

_____
_____
_____
_____
_____


What part of the potato plant do you eat? _____

Why shouldn't you eat the green leafy part? _____

What type of soil do potatoes grow best in? _____


Research and find a recipe for Needhams and make it. What is the main ingredient in this candy? What other candy recipes can you find using potatoes? _____

_____
_____
_____

# HEALTH/PHYSICAL EDUCATION

Either with potatoes you've grown or purchased at the grocery store, see how many recipes you can come up with for different ways to prepare potatoes. Consider using *101 Things to Do with a Potato* by Stephanie Ashcroft. List your ideas below.

_____
_____
_____
_____
_____
_____
_____
_____
_____
_____

Create sacks like those potatoes were originally taken to market in, and have a sack race. Younger students could use king sized pillow cases for this activity. Sacks can be purchased at hardware and feed stores. Post a picture of you participating in the sack race below.

# COMPUTER/LIBRARY SKILLS

You will use the internet and/or your local library for a great deal of the research for this unit study. List the various resources you used during the course of your study.

Source Title                                                                    Type of Media

_____

_____

_____

_____

_____

_____

_____

_____

_____

_____

_____

_____

_____

_____

_____

_____

_____

_____

_____

_____

_____

_____

_____

_____

_____

_____

_____

_____

_____

_____

_____

_____

_____

_____

_____

# FINE ARTS

Make Mr. Potato Heads using real potatoes and other fruits and vegetable.  Take pictures for your portfolio.

Cut potatoes in half and create potato stamp images to make greeting cards.  Websites like this one will show you how, http://www.diynetwork.com/how-to/make-and-decorate/crafts/how-to-use-a-potato-to-make-greeting-cards

For older students, look up Vincent van Gogh, find a picture of his painting called "The Potato Eaters" and study it closely.  Research what the artist was trying to portray in his painting.  Then take time to observe your own evening meal with your family.  Make a sketch of your mealtime.  Include your family members, where they were seated, what was on the table and the room where you were eating.  Choose another medium (colored pencils, pastels, paint) and create a finished work of art from your sketch.

# MAINE STUDIES

Read "The Joy of Digging Potatoes" at this link:
https://www.almanac.com/news/almanac/musings/joy-digging-potatoes

Pretend you are one of the children that gets to participate in picking the potatoes. Write your own story about your day in the field. What time of year is it? How do you feel when you find a potato? What are the smells and sounds around you? Who is in the field picking with you? Are you digging the potatoes, or picking them up after a harvester goes through the field? Describe the celebration you will have when the harvest is over.

_____

_____

_____

_____

_____

_____

_____

_____

_____

_____

_____

_____

_____

_____

_____

_____

_____

_____

_____

_____

_____

_____

_____

_____

_____

_____

_____

**FIELD TRIPS**

Visit Get Real, Get Maine (www.getrealmaine.com) to find a farm that grows potatoes near you, and contact them about arranging a possible field trip.

Plan to attend the Fort Fairfield Potato Blossom Festival in July.

If you can't visit a potato farm in person, watch one of the videos at the links below to learn more about how potatoes grow.

https://www.youtube.com/watch?v=HEtdFHlcGBU

https://www.youtube.com/watch?v=fmuueelyQww

https://www.youtube.com/watch?v=9xiJct0dw3k

What did you learn about how potatoes grow? _____

_____

_____

_____

_____

_____

_____

_____

_____

Draw something you learned about how potatoes grow.

## What I Learned

In this section, ask the student to narrate what they learned that they didn't know when they began this study. What new discovery did they make during the study? What did they enjoy most? What do they know now that they didn't know before? These are all good questions to ask, if the student needs prompting.

_____
_____
_____
_____
_____
_____
_____
_____
_____
_____
_____
_____
_____
_____
_____
_____
_____
_____
_____
_____
_____
_____

Date Completed: _____

# Harvest the Sea:  Lobster and Seaweed

www.homeschoolersofmaine.org

# Table of Contents

www.homeschoolersofmaine.org

## Before You Begin

Sometimes it can be challenging to figure out how to show progress when a student is working on a unit study. Before you begin this study, ask the student to give you a brief narrative of what they already know about the subject. Write this out for younger students, and have older students write it out for themselves, here. When you finish the study, there is a page at the end entitled **What I Learned** for students to write down new things that they learned during the study. The comparison of these two pages can be used for portfolio reviews to document that progress in learning was made by the student.

_____
_____
_____
_____
_____
_____
_____
_____
_____
_____
_____
_____
_____
_____
_____
_____
_____
_____
_____
_____
_____
_____
_____
_____
_____
_____
_____

Date Begun: _____

**BIBLE**

If a person adheres to the Levitical Law (Leviticus 11:12), would eating lobster be permissible? Why or why not?

_____
_____
_____
_____
_____

On what day of the creation story were lobsters created? Every creature has a role or purpose. Based on where they live and what they eat, what role do you think the lobster plays in the ocean ecosystem?

_____
_____
_____
_____
_____

On what day of the creation story was seaweed created?

_____
_____
_____
_____
_____

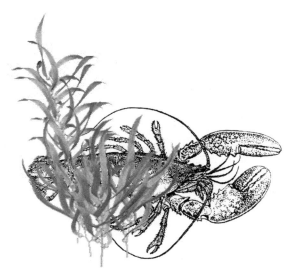

# MATH

What are the dimensions of a lobster trap?  Why are these the dimensions used?

_____

_____

_____

_____

_____


What is the length of a legal lobster?  Why isn't it legal to keep lobsters that are smaller or larger than this size?

_____

_____

_____

_____

_____


What math skills might a lobsterman need?  List them below.

_____

_____

_____

_____

_____


How much meat can you expect to get from a lobster that weighs 1.25 pounds? _____

Subtract that from the total weight of the lobster. How much did the shell weigh? _____

How many lobsters would you need to get 1 pound of lobster meat? _____

What is the current price of a 1 pound lobster? _____

What is the current price of 1 pound of lobster meat? _____

Would it be more or less expensive to buy enough lobsters to pick your own pound of lobster meat? _____

How much more/less would it cost? _____

## LANGUAGE ARTS

Read the stories *Star Island Boy* by Louise Dickenson Rich and *Touch Blue* by Cynthia Lord.  Compare and contrast the stories.

_____
_____
_____
_____
_____
_____

Write a story about a lobster living on the Maine coast among the seaweed.  What does a lobster's day look like?  What do they eat?  Who are their friends?  Who are their enemies?  What do they think about the shadows cast by the lobster boats and the big metal boxes that drop into the sea with food in them?

_____
_____
_____
_____
_____
_____
_____
_____
_____
_____

What is an adjective?  Find out more about Maine seaweed, and list five adjectives that describe this plant.  Now write a descriptive sentence about seaweed using some or all of the adjectives from your list.

1. _____

2. _____

3. _____

4. _____

5. _____

_____
_____
_____

# SOCIAL STUDIES

Lobsters then and now:  Research how this now delicacy was once considered food for the poor and indigent.  What changed?

_____
_____
_____
_____
_____

List as many things as you can think of (or find through research), that a lobsterman will need in order to go fishing.

_____
_____
_____
_____
_____
_____
_____

September 25 is National Lobster Day.  Plan a lobster themed celebration for the day.

Describe your celebration below.

_____
_____
_____
_____
_____
_____
_____
_____
_____

www.homeschoolersofmaine.org

# SCIENCE

Define crustacean.  What is the Maine state crustacean?

_____

_____

_____

_____

Read *The Blue Lobster:  A Life Cycle* by Carol Carrick.  Are blue lobsters real?  Why are they blue?  What else does the story tell about lobsters that you didn't know before you read it?

_____

_____

_____

_____

_____

Find out how to tell if a lobster is male or female.

_____

_____

_____

_____

_____

How many eggs does a typical one pound female carry?  _____

Are lobsters herbivore, carnivore or omnivore? Explain your answer.  _____

_____

_____

Why do lobstermen cut a "V" notch into the tail of some lobsters and not others?  What happens if a lobsterman catches a lobster with a "V" notch in its tail?

_____

_____

_____

_____

_____

Visit Gulf of Maine Research Institute online to learn more about lobsters.  www.gma.org/lobsters.index.html.

Learn to identify the different types of seaweed in Maine. Visit a beach and put a checkmark next to the ones you discovered.

| | |
|---|---|
| ____ Rockweed | ____ Winged Kelp |
| ____ Wormweed | ____ Dulse |
| ____ Bladderwrack | ____ Irish Moss |
| ____ Sugar Kelp | ____ Laver |
| ____ Horsetail Kelp | ____ Sea Lettuce |

## HEALTH/PHYSICAL EDUCATION

What is the science behind the reason that God declared some animals, like lobsters and pigs, to be unclean?

_____

_____

_____

_____

_____

What are the health benefits of eating seaweed?  Do different types have different benefits?

_____

_____

_____

_____

_____

Visit Vitamin Seaweed (http://www.vitaminseaseaweed.com/) or Maine Coast Sea Vegetables (https://www.seaveg.com) to learn more about harvesting vegetables from the ocean and their health benefits. What did you learn.

_____

_____

_____

_____

_____

# COMPUTER/LIBRARY SKILLS

You will use the internet and/or your local library for a great deal of the research for this unit study. List the various resources you used during the course of your study.

Source Title                                                    Type of Media

_____

_____

_____

_____

_____

_____

_____

_____

_____

_____

_____

_____

_____

_____

_____

_____

_____

_____

_____

_____

_____

_____

_____

_____

_____

_____

_____

_____

## FINE ARTS

Read *Lobsterman* by Dahlov Ipcar.  Plan a visit to the Farnsworth Marine Museum in Rockland to view her work. Pretend you are an art critic. Write an article describing the art.

_____

_____

_____

_____

_____

_____

_____

_____

_____

# MAINE STUDIES

In order to obtain a fishing license for lobstering in Maine, you must participate in the lobstering apprenticeship program. Research the apprenticeship program and write what you learned?

_____
_____
_____
_____
_____
_____
_____
_____

Research and write your own brief history of lobstering in Maine? _____

_____
_____
_____
_____
_____
_____
_____
_____

What other foods are  harvested from the Atlantic Ocean in or around Maine?

_____
_____
_____
_____
_____
_____

# FIELD TRIPS

Take a trip to the Maine State Aquarium.  What did you see? Is there something you discovered that you never knew existed? Write about it below.

_____

_____

_____

_____

_____

Take a trip to Penobscot Marine Museum.

_____

_____

_____

_____

_____

Visit the local grocery store and check out the lobster tank in the meat department.

_____

_____

_____

_____

_____

Plan a trip to Rockland for the Maine Lobster Festival during the first week in August.  On opening day, general admission tickets are $1 for adults and free for kids ages 6 – 12.  Find out more here: http://www.mainelobsterfestival.com/.

# What I Learned

In this section, ask the student to narrate what they learned that they didn't know when they began this study. What new discovery did they make during the study? What did they enjoy most? What do they know now that they didn't know before? These are all good questions to ask, if the student needs prompting.

_____
_____
_____
_____
_____
_____
_____
_____
_____
_____
_____
_____
_____
_____
_____
_____
_____
_____
_____
_____
_____
_____
_____
_____
_____
_____
_____
_____
_____

Date Completed: _____

# Pancakes:

# A Unit Study on Blueberries and Maple Syrup

## Table of Contents

## Before You Begin

Sometimes it can be challenging to figure out how to show progress when a student is working on a unit study. Before you begin this study, ask the student to give you a brief narrative of what they already know about the subject. Write this out for younger students, and have older students write it out for themselves, here. When you finish the study, there is a page at the end entitled **What I Learned** for students to write down new things that they learned during the study. The comparison of these two pages can be used for portfolio reviews to document that progress in learning was made by the student.

_____
_____
_____
_____
_____
_____
_____
_____
_____
_____
_____
_____
_____
_____
_____
_____
_____
_____
_____
_____
_____
_____
_____
_____
_____
_____
_____

Date Begun: _____

# BIBLE

Watch Veggie Tales *Madame Blueberry Learns to Be Thankful*. Keep a gratitude journal for the duration of this study, listing at least three things each day that you are thankful for.

1. _____

2. _____

3. _____


Read the following verses and answer the questions.

**Why do we give thanks?**

Psalm 7:17, Psalm 106:1 _____


**How are we to give thanks?**

Psalm 9:1 _____


**When should we give thanks?**

Philippians 4:6-7, 1 Thessalonians 5:16-18 _____


What do you think it means to give thanks in every situation? _____

_____

_____

_____

_____

_____

www.homeschoolersofmaine.org

# MATH

Find the answers to the following:

An average maple tree produces _____ sap per day.

_____ gallons of sap are needed to produce one quart of syrup.

Calculate how much maple syrup your family uses over a period of one month. Multiply that by 12 to estimate how much your family would use in one year.

_____

How many gallons of sap would be required to produce the amount of syrup your family consumes?

_____

Plan to tap trees during the next maple season. Pick several trees to compare. Create a graph that reflects how much sap was collected from each tree.

| # of Gallons | Tree 1 | Tree 2 | Tree 3 | Tree 4 | Tree 5 |
|---|---|---|---|---|---|
|  |  |  |  |  |  |
|  |  |  |  |  |  |
|  |  |  |  |  |  |
|  |  |  |  |  |  |
|  |  |  |  |  |  |
|  |  |  |  |  |  |
|  |  |  |  |  |  |
|  |  |  |  |  |  |
|  |  |  |  |  |  |

Visit the local grocery store and find out how much one quart of Maine maple syrup costs. Try to find pints of syrup from Vermont, Canada and Maine and compare the prices.

                        Cost

Maine Maple Syrup        _____

Canadian Maple Syrup     _____

Vermont Maple Syrup      _____


Is the cost of Maine maple syrup more or less than the cost of syrup from other locations? _____


How much does a pint of fresh blueberries cost? How much does a quart cost? Is it less expensive to pick your own or to have someone else pick them for you? What do you think the reason is for this?

_____

_____

_____

_____


How many blueberries does it take to make a batch of blueberry muffins for your family? _____

How many blueberries does it take to make blueberry muffins for your family for one meal? _____

If you made muffins once a week and pancakes twice a week, how many blueberries would you need? _____

How much would it cost to buy the blueberries fresh? _____

How much would it cost to buy the same amount of frozen Maine blueberries? _____

Which costs more, the fresh or frozen blueberries? _____

How much more do they cost? _____

# LANGUAGE ARTS

Consider reading one (or all) of the following books.

_____ *If You Give a Pig a Pancake* by Laura Numeroff

_____ *Pancakes, Pancakes* by Eric Carle

_____ *Pancakes for Breakfast* by Tomie de Paola

_____ *Sheldon's Lunch* by Bruce Lemerise

_____ *Blueberries for Sal* by Robert McClosky

Which book(s) did you read?  What did you like best/least about it?  Would you recommend it to a friend? Why or why not?

_____

_____

_____

_____

_____

_____

_____

Write a story to go with the pictures in Tomie de Paola's book *Pancakes for Breakfast*.

_____

_____

_____

_____

_____

_____

_____

_____

_____

_____

_____

_____

_____

_____

_____

_____

www.homeschoolersofmaine.org

# SOCIAL STUDIES

Attend a local pancake breakfast.  Volunteer to help serve others. Write about it.  Format your writing as if it were an article in a newspaper.

_____

_____

_____

_____

_____

_____

_____

What organization in your community hosted the pancake breakfast? _____

_____

Learn more about the organization and share what you learned?  Be sure to include the organizations name and what impact they have on your community? Where do the funds go that were raised by holding the breakfast?

_____

_____

_____

_____

How much of Maine's annual income is generated by the maple industry?  The blueberry industry?  Do these industries significantly impact the overall economy of the State?  What happens in a year where the sap production is low or the blueberry crop is smaller than normal?

_____

_____

_____

_____

_____

_____

_____

Learn more about the history of blueberries, here:
https://umainetoday.umaine.edu/2019/03/18/blueberry-history/

## SCIENCE

Research and learn about the steps involved in producing maple sugar from maple sap. Use what you've learned to make a batch of maple sugar at home. List the steps below.

_____

_____

_____

_____

_____

_____

_____

What type of tree does sap come from that is used to make the syrup you put on your pancakes?

_____

Learn to identify the tree by its bark and leaf. Find a tree in your neighborhood that produces sap for syrup. Create a tree rubbing of the bark by placing a piece of paper on the bark of the tree and coloring on the paper with a crayon. Be sure to include it in your nature journal. Draw a picture of the leaf below.

Learn more about Maine maple syrup and those who produce it here:
http://mainemapleproducers.com/

Investigate why Maine blueberries continue to be harvested by hand when most crops are now harvested by machine. Find a blueberry grower who invites the public to rake and try raking blueberries. Write a brief description of your experience, what you saw, heard, smelled, felt during the process.

_____
_____
_____
_____
_____
_____
_____
_____
_____
_____

Learn more about Maine blueberries here:
https://extension.umaine.edu/blueberries/

Make pancakes from scratch. Cooking is chemistry. If the ingredients aren't added in the right proportions, you won't create what you're trying to achieve. Find a pancake recipe online, or use a family favorite, and make pancakes. Be sure to add blueberries and top with maple syrup. Which of the ingredients that you used make the pancakes fluffy? What other ingredients, besides blueberries can you add to your pancakes? Experiment with different recipes. Which recipe did you like best? Why?

_____
_____
_____
_____
_____
_____
_____
_____
_____
_____
_____
_____
_____

## HEALTH/PHYSICAL EDUCATION

Wild Maine blueberries are reportedly higher in antioxidants than other blueberries. What is an antioxidant? Why would wild Maine blueberries be higher in this than other blueberries?

_____

_____

_____

_____

Research whether or not there are health benefits to maple syrup. What do you think based on what you've learned? Is maple syrup good for you? Why or why not?

_____

_____

_____

_____

_____

Plan a late July or early August hike during blueberry season in a park where blueberries grow. Be sure to check with the park before you go. There may be different rules regarding picking and raking, depending on the park.

_____

_____

_____

_____

# COMPUTER/LIBRARY SKILLS

You will use the internet and/or your local library for a great deal of the research for this unit study. List the various resources you used during the course of your study.

Source Title                                                    Type of Media

_____

_____

_____

_____

_____

_____

_____

_____

_____

_____

_____

_____

_____

_____

_____

_____

_____

_____

_____

_____

_____

_____

_____

_____

_____

_____

_____

_____

_____

www.homeschoolersofmaine.org

## FINE ARTS

Research the work and life of Hall Groat II.  Study his work *Blueberry Pancakes and Maple Syrup*.

What medium does he typically use in his work? _____

What medium did he use for this work? _____

What other works has he done? _____

_____

_____

_____

Replicate his work using your favorite medium: acrylic, oil, watercolor, clay, photography, etc.

Make a blueberry pie. Check out the pie crust art at this link and create your won fancy crust for your pie.
https://www.tasteofhome.com/article/how-to-make-decorative-pie-crusts/

Post a picture of one of your creations below.

# MAINE STUDIES

How does Maine rank in the United States in blueberry production? _____

What are the two types of blueberries that grow wild in Maine? _____

How does Maine rank in the nation in maple syrup production? _____

What county in Maine produces the most maple syrup? _____


Blueberries for Sal takes place in Maine. Though the author isn't from Maine, he summered here. Research Robert McCloskey's life and write a brief report.

_____
_____
_____
_____
_____
_____
_____
_____
_____
_____
_____
_____
_____
_____
_____
_____


Did he write other books that take place in Maine? If so, what are they?

_____
_____
_____
_____
_____
_____
_____
_____
_____
_____

**FIELD TRIPS**

Various field trip opportunities are mentioned throughout the study.  These include, but are not limited to:

_____ Visit a Sugar Shack on Maine Maple Sunday, which is typically the 4th Sunday in March each year.

_____ Attend the local blueberry festival.

_____ Attend a local pancake breakfast.

_____ Go blueberry raking.

# Field Trip Form

**Date:** _____

**Destination:** _____

**Purpose:** _____

**Write about your trip below:**

_____

_____

_____

_____

_____

_____

_____

_____

**Did you learn anything new from your visit?** _____

_____

_____

**Draw a picture showing something you did or learned.**

# What I Learned

In this section, ask the student to narrate what they learned that they didn't know when they began this study. What new discovery did they make during the study? What did they enjoy most? What do they know now that they didn't know before? These are all good questions to ask, if the student needs prompting.

_____
_____
_____
_____
_____
_____
_____
_____
_____
_____
_____
_____
_____
_____
_____
_____
_____
_____
_____
_____
_____
_____
_____
_____
_____
_____
_____
_____

Date Completed: _____

Made in the USA
Las Vegas, NV
28 March 2022